Warm regards,

FAISAL JAMIL

I Always Give's Free Copies Need Your Feedback And

Reviews Keeps In Touch!

http://www.amazon.com/author/faisal.jamil

Email: faisaljamilauthor@gmail.com

About the author

Certainly! Faisal Jamil is a multifaceted individual with a diverse set of skills and experiences. With a strong foundation in computer knowledge since childhood, he has developed a deep understanding of technology that informs his work as a content writer. Faisal also possesses digital skills, which further enhance his abilities in various digital platforms and technologies.

Beyond his professional endeavors, Faisal Jamil has also excelled in the martial arts, particularly Shotokan Karate, where he achieved the prestigious rank of first Dan black belt. This achievement speaks to his dedication, discipline, and commitment to personal growth and mastery.

In his professional life, Faisal Jamil has carved out a successful career in sales management within the Fast Moving Consumer Goods (FMCG) sector. His roles in various FMCG companies have honed his skills in strategic planning, team leadership, and business development. Faisal's ability to drive sales and achieve targets has been instrumental in his career progression, showcasing his talent for identifying opportunities and delivering results.

Faisal Jamil is also deeply interested in business investment strategies, planning, and execution. His understanding of these areas has been key to his success in the business world, allowing him to make informed decisions and implement effective strategies. His ability to navigate the complexities of investment planning and execution has set him apart as a strategic thinker and a valuable asset in any business endeavor.

Overall, Faisal Jamil is a dynamic individual who combines his passion for technology, martial arts, sales management, digital skills, and business investment strategies to achieve success in diverse fields. His journey is a testament to his versatility, resilience, and continuous pursuit of excellence.

Yours Sincerely

FAISAL JAMIL

I Always Give's Free Copies Need Your Feedback And

Reviews Keeps In Touch!

https://www.amazon.com/author/faisal.jamil

Email: faisaljamilauthor@gmail.com

HOW ALGORITHMS WORK ON

YOUTUBE

Table of Content

Preface --9

Introduction --11

Chapter 1: Introduction to YouTube Algorithms ----------15

1.1 The Evolution of YouTube Algorithms --------------------15

1.2 Basic Concepts of Algorithms --------------------------------18

1.3 The Purpose of YouTube Algorithms ----------------------20

Chapter 2: Video Discovery and Recommendations ------22

2.1 How the Recommendation System Works --------------22

2.2 Personalization and User Profiling ------------------------25

2.3 Continuous Learning and Adaptation --------------------27

Chapter 3: Search Algorithms ----------------------------------30

3.1 Understanding YouTube Search --------------------------30

3.2 Keyword Optimization and Metadata --------------------32

3.3 User Intent and Contextual Relevance ------------------35

Chapter 4: Engagement Metrics and Ranking --------------38

4.1 Key Engagement Metrics ------------------------------------38

4.2 Watch Time and Session Duration ------------------------40

4.3 User Interaction Signals ------------------------------------42

Chapter 5: Content Quality and Creator Reputation -----45

5.1 Assessing Content Quality ----------------------------------45

5.2 Building Creator Reputation -------------------------------47

5.3 Handling Content Violations and Demonetization ----50

Chapter 6: Audience Development and Growth ----------53

6.1 Audience Retention Strategies ----------------------------53

6.2 Subscriber Growth and Engagement --------------------56

6.3 Community Building and Interaction --------------------58

Chapter 7: Algorithmic Impact on Video Promotion -----61

7.1 Trends and Virality ---61

7.2 Cross-Promotions and Collaborations --------------------64

7.3 Paid Promotions and Advertisements --------------------66

Chapter 8: Algorithm Transparency and Criticism --------69

8.1 Transparency Efforts by YouTube -------------------------69

8.2 Common Criticisms of YouTube Algorithms ------------72

8.3 Balancing Algorithmic Decisions --------------------------75

Chapter 9: Future of YouTube Algorithms ------------------78

9.1 Emerging Technologies in Algorithm Development ---78

9.2 User Privacy and Data Ethics --------------------------------80

9.3 Anticipating Future Trends ----------------------------------82

Chapter 10: Practical Tips for Navigating

YouTube Algorithms ---86

10.1 Staying Updated with Algorithm Changes -------------86

10.2 Practical Optimization Techniques ---------------------88

10.3 Building a Resilient Content Strategy -------------------90

Closing of the book --93

Description of the book ---95

Preface

Welcome to **"How Algorithms Work on YouTube"**, a comprehensive guide designed to unravel the complexities behind YouTube's algorithmic engine. In an age where digital content is king, understanding how algorithms shape the discovery, promotion, and success of videos is crucial for creators, marketers, and enthusiasts alike.

Since its inception, YouTube has evolved from a simple video-sharing platform to a sophisticated ecosystem driven by powerful algorithms. These algorithms determine what content gets seen, how it is ranked, and ultimately, how creators can achieve success on the platform. This book aims to demystify these processes, providing you with the knowledge and tools needed to navigate and thrive in this dynamic environment.

The journey begins with an exploration of the evolution of YouTube's algorithms, tracing their development from basic popularity metrics to the complex machine learning models used today. We delve into the core concepts of algorithms, their role in the digital age, and the purposes they serve in enhancing user experiences and maximizing engagement.

From there, we dive into the specifics of video discovery and recommendations, shedding light on how YouTube tailors content to individual users through sophisticated recommendation systems and personalization techniques. You'll learn about the critical role of search algorithms, keyword optimization, and metadata in ensuring your content reaches the right audience.

Engagement metrics and ranking factors are vital to understanding how videos are prioritized on YouTube. This book provides a thorough analysis of key engagement metrics, the significance of watch time, and the impact of user interaction signals. We also examine how content quality and creator reputation influence algorithmic decisions and explore strategies for building a strong and sustainable presence on the platform.

In addition to these core topics, we address the broader implications of YouTube's algorithms, including transparency efforts, common criticisms, and the ethical considerations surrounding user privacy and data protection. Looking to the future, we explore emerging technologies, anticipate trends in content consumption, and offer practical tips for staying updated and optimizing your content.

"How Algorithms Work on YouTube" is not just a technical manual; it is a strategic guide to building a resilient content strategy that can adapt to the ever-changing digital landscape. Whether you are a seasoned creator or just starting your YouTube journey, this book is designed to equip you with the insights and strategies needed to succeed.

Thank you for embarking on this journey with us. We hope this book empowers you to harness the full potential of YouTube's algorithms and achieve your creative and professional goals.

Sincerely,

FAISAL JAMIL

INTRODUCTION

Welcome to **"How Algorithms Work on YouTube"**, a detailed exploration of the intricate systems that govern the world's most popular video-sharing platform. This book is designed to give you a thorough understanding of how YouTube's algorithms function and how they impact video visibility, user engagement, and content success.

The Importance of Algorithms

Algorithms are the backbone of YouTube, dictating what content gets recommended, how search results are ranked, and how users interact with the platform. For creators, understanding these algorithms is essential for optimizing content, growing an audience, and achieving long-term success. For viewers, these algorithms shape the experience by tailoring content to individual preferences and habits.

Evolution and Complexity

Since YouTube's launch in 2005, its algorithms have evolved significantly. Initially, the platform relied on basic popularity metrics like views and uploads. Today, it uses sophisticated machine learning models that analyze a vast array of data points to deliver personalized content to over two billion monthly active users. This evolution has been driven by advancements in technology and a deepening understanding of user behavior.

Purpose and Functionality

At its core, YouTube's algorithmic system aims to enhance user experience by providing relevant and engaging content. It strives to maximize engagement and retention, balancing user satisfaction with the platform's business objectives. Understanding how these algorithms work is key to leveraging them effectively, whether you're a content creator, marketer, or viewer.

What This Book Covers

In this book, we break down the complexities of YouTube's algorithms into manageable sections:

Chapter 1: Introduction to YouTube Algorithms:

We start by tracing the evolution of YouTube's algorithms and exploring their basic concepts and purposes.

Chapter 2: Video Discovery and Recommendations:

This chapter dives into the recommendation system, personalization techniques, and the continuous learning process of algorithms.

Chapter 3: Search Algorithms:

Understand the inner workings of YouTube's search engine, including keyword optimization and the role of user intent.

Chapter 4: Engagement Metrics and Ranking:

Learn about key engagement metrics, the significance of watch time, and how user interaction signals influence ranking.

Chapter 5: Content Quality and Creator Reputation:

Explore how algorithms assess content quality, build creator reputation, and handle content violations.

Chapter 6: Audience Development and Growth:

Discover strategies for audience retention, subscriber growth, and community building.

Chapter 7: Algorithmic Impact on Video Promotion:

Understand how algorithms detect trends, the role of cross-promotions and collaborations, and the impact of paid promotions.

Chapter 8: Algorithm Transparency and Criticism:

Analyze YouTube's efforts to increase transparency, common criticisms, and the balancing act of algorithmic decisions.

Chapter 9: Future of YouTube Algorithms:

Look ahead at emerging technologies, user privacy, data ethics, and future trends in content consumption.

Chapter 10: Practical Tips for Navigating YouTube

Algorithms:

Get practical advice on staying updated with algorithm changes, optimizing content, and building a resilient content strategy.

Your Journey with This Book

Whether you're a seasoned content creator or new to YouTube, this book is designed to provide you with actionable insights and strategies. By understanding the mechanics of YouTube's algorithms, you can better navigate the platform, optimize your content, and engage your audience effectively.

Thank you for choosing this book as your guide to mastering YouTube's algorithms. Let's embark on this journey together, unlocking the secrets of one of the most powerful digital platforms in the world.

Sincerely,

FAISAL JAMIL

Chapter 1
Introduction to
YouTube Algorithms

1.1 The Evolution of YouTube Algorithms

The journey from basic popularity metrics to complex

machine learning models

When YouTube first launched in 2005, its video ranking system was relatively simple. The primary metric for determining the popularity of a video was the number of views it received. This basic approach, while straightforward, had significant limitations. It didn't account for the quality of views—whether users were actually engaging with the content or simply clicking on the video and then quickly leaving.

As YouTube grew, so did the need for a more sophisticated system to manage its vast library of content and improve user experience. By 2012, YouTube began to place greater emphasis on watch time rather than just view counts. This shift acknowledged that the amount of time viewers spent watching videos was a better indicator of content quality and user engagement. The introduction of watch time as a key metric marked the beginning of YouTube's transition to more complex algorithmic models.

Over the years, YouTube's algorithms have evolved from these simple metrics to incorporate advanced machine learning models. These models analyze vast amounts of data to predict user preferences and recommend content that is most likely to keep users engaged. The algorithms now consider a multitude of factors, including watch history, search queries, likes, dislikes, comments, and more. This complexity allows for a highly personalized user experience, where recommendations are tailored to the unique preferences of each individual user.

Key milestones in the development of YouTube's algorithms

Several key milestones have shaped the development of YouTube's algorithms:

2005-2011: View Counts and Basic Engagement Metrics

Initially, YouTube relied on simple metrics like view counts and the number of likes and dislikes. This period saw the growth of clickbait titles and thumbnails as creators sought to maximize clicks.

2012: Introduction of Watch Time

In an effort to prioritize content that retained viewer attention, YouTube introduced watch time as a crucial metric. Videos that kept viewers engaged for longer periods began to be ranked higher.

2016: Machine Learning and Deep Learning Models

YouTube began leveraging advanced machine learning techniques, including deep learning, to analyze user behavior and improve content recommendations.

This period marked the start of more personalized recommendations.

2018: Changes to Combat Misinformation and Improve Quality

In response to criticism about the spread of misinformation and harmful content, YouTube implemented changes to its algorithms to prioritize authoritative sources, particularly in search results and recommendations.

2021: Increased Focus on Shorts and New Content Formats

With the rise of short-form video content, YouTube adapted its algorithms to accommodate and promote YouTube Shorts, ensuring that these new formats received appropriate visibility.

The role of user feedback and technological advancements

User feedback has been instrumental in shaping YouTube's algorithms. The platform continually collects data on user interactions, such as watch time, likes, dislikes, comments, and shares. This data helps YouTube understand what types of content users enjoy and engage with the most. Additionally, YouTube conducts surveys and experiments to gather qualitative feedback directly from users.

Technological advancements, particularly in the fields of artificial intelligence and machine learning, have played a critical role in the evolution of YouTube's algorithms. The development of neural networks and deep learning models has enabled YouTube to process and analyze vast amounts of data with remarkable accuracy. These technologies allow the algorithms to identify patterns in user behavior and make highly accurate predictions about what content users are likely to enjoy.

1.2 Basic Concepts of Algorithms

Definition and types of algorithms

An algorithm is a set of instructions or rules designed to perform a specific task or solve a particular problem. In the context of computing, algorithms are used to process data and make decisions based on that data. There are several types of algorithms, including:

Sorting Algorithms

These algorithms arrange data in a particular order. Examples include quicksort, mergesort, and bubble sort.

Search Algorithms

These algorithms are used to find specific data within a dataset. Examples include binary search and linear search.

Machine Learning Algorithms

These algorithms enable computers to learn from data and make predictions or decisions without being explicitly programmed. Examples include decision trees, neural networks, and support vector machines.

Recommendation Algorithms

These algorithms suggest content or products to users based on their preferences and behavior. YouTube's recommendation system is an example of this type.

How algorithms process data and make decisions

Algorithms process data through a series of steps, transforming raw input into meaningful output. In the case of YouTube's algorithms, the process typically involves the following stages:

Data Collection

Algorithms collect data from various sources, including user interactions (e.g., watch history, likes, comments) and video metadata (e.g., titles, descriptions, tags).

Data Analysis

The collected data is analyzed to identify patterns and correlations. For example, algorithms might analyze which types of videos a user watches frequently or how long they watch certain videos.

Model Training

Machine learning models are trained on the analyzed data. During this phase, the models learn to make predictions based on historical data.

Decision Making

Once trained, the models use real-time data to make decisions. For YouTube, this involves recommending videos that are likely to keep users engaged.

Feedback Loop

The algorithms continually update and refine their models based on new data and user interactions, ensuring that recommendations remain relevant and accurate.

The importance of algorithms in the digital age

Algorithms are essential in the digital age for several reasons:

Personalization

Algorithms enable personalized experiences by tailoring content and recommendations to individual preferences. This enhances user satisfaction and engagement.

Efficiency

Algorithms can process vast amounts of data quickly and accurately, making it possible to deliver relevant content in real-time.

Scalability

Algorithms allow platforms like YouTube to manage and deliver content to millions of users simultaneously, something that would be impossible with manual curation.

Innovation

Advances in algorithmic technologies drive innovation in various fields, including artificial intelligence, healthcare, finance, and entertainment.

1.3 The Purpose of YouTube Algorithms

Enhancing user experience through personalized content

One of the primary purposes of YouTube's algorithms is to enhance the user experience by delivering personalized content. By analyzing individual user behavior, preferences, and interactions, YouTube's algorithms can recommend videos that are most likely to interest each user. This personalization ensures that users spend more time on the platform, discovering content that aligns with their tastes and interests.

Maximizing engagement and retention

YouTube's algorithms aim to maximize user engagement and retention. By recommending videos that keep users watching for longer periods, the platform can increase overall watch time and encourage repeat visits. High engagement levels are beneficial for both YouTube and content creators, as they lead to more ad impressions, higher ad revenue, and greater visibility for videos.

Balancing user satisfaction with business objectives

While enhancing user experience and maximizing engagement are crucial, YouTube's algorithms also need to balance these goals with the platform's business objectives. This includes optimizing ad placements to generate revenue, promoting content from partners and advertisers, and ensuring that the platform remains a safe and trustworthy environment for users.

YouTube's algorithms must navigate this complex landscape, making decisions that satisfy user needs while also meeting business targets. This balancing act involves continuously refining algorithms to align with evolving user behaviors, content trends, and market dynamics.

Chapter 2
Video Discovery and Recommendations

2.1 How the Recommendation System Works

The underlying technology of the recommendation engine

YouTube's recommendation system is powered by sophisticated machine learning algorithms designed to process vast amounts of data and deliver personalized content suggestions. The core technology involves a combination of collaborative filtering, content-based filtering, and deep learning models.

Collaborative Filtering

This technique analyzes user behavior to identify patterns and similarities among users. By examining the viewing habits of users with similar preferences, YouTube can recommend videos that others in the same group have enjoyed. For instance, if User A and User B have similar watch histories, videos that User A has watched and liked are likely to be recommended to User B.

Content-Based Filtering

This method focuses on the content of the videos themselves. By analyzing metadata, such as titles, descriptions, tags, and transcripts, the algorithm identifies videos that are similar in content to those a user has previously watched. If a user frequently watches cooking videos, the algorithm will recommend more videos within that genre.

Deep Learning Models

Deep learning involves neural networks that mimic the human brain's functioning. These models process complex patterns in data, including video thumbnails, user comments, and even the visual and audio elements of videos. Deep learning allows the recommendation system to make highly accurate predictions about what videos a user might enjoy based on nuanced aspects of content and user interactions.

Factors influencing video recommendations

Several factors influence the recommendations that YouTube's algorithms generate:

Watch History

The most significant factor is a user's watch history. The algorithm analyzes the types of videos a user has watched in the past, how long they watched them, and how frequently they return to similar content.

Engagement Metrics

Likes, dislikes, shares, comments, and subscriptions are critical indicators of a user's preferences. Videos with high engagement from a user's activity are more likely to be recommended.

Search Queries

The algorithm considers recent search queries to understand a user's current interests and recommend videos that align with those search terms.

User Interactions

Clicking on thumbnails, adding videos to playlists, and other forms of interaction provide valuable data that the algorithm uses to refine recommendations.

Video Metadata

Information such as titles, descriptions, tags, and closed captions helps the algorithm categorize and recommend content accurately.

Trending and Popular Content

Current trends and popular videos within the broader community can influence recommendations, especially if the user shows interest in similar trending content.

The impact of watch history and user behavior

Watch history and user behavior play a crucial role in shaping recommendations. Here's how:

Watch Duration

The amount of time a user spends watching a video is a strong indicator of interest. Videos that are watched in their entirety or for extended periods are given more weight in the recommendation algorithm.

Frequency of Views

Repeated viewing of similar types of videos indicates a strong preference, prompting the algorithm to recommend more of the same genre or topic.

Engagement Patterns

The way users interact with videos—such as liking, commenting, or sharing—provides signals about their preferences. High engagement with specific types of content informs the algorithm to recommend similar videos.

User Feedback

Direct feedback, such as marking a video as "Not Interested," helps the algorithm refine future recommendations, ensuring that irrelevant content is filtered out.

2.2 Personalization and User Profiling

Methods for creating user profiles based on interactions

Creating user profiles involves aggregating data from various interactions to build a comprehensive picture of a user's preferences. Methods include:

Behavioral Analysis

Tracking user activities, such as the types of videos watched, the duration of views, and the frequency of interactions, helps in creating detailed behavioral profiles.

Demographic Data

Information such as age, gender, location, and language preferences is used to refine recommendations and ensure relevance.

Content Interaction

The algorithm monitors how users interact with different content types (e.g., likes, comments, shares) to identify their interests and preferences.

Cross-Platform Data

For users who are logged in across multiple devices, YouTube aggregates data from all platforms to create a unified user profile.

Tailoring recommendations to individual preferences

Once a user profile is established, recommendations are tailored using several techniques:

Contextual Relevance

The algorithm considers the context of the user's current session, including recent searches and the time of day, to provide timely and relevant recommendations.

Content Diversity

To avoid repetitive suggestions, the algorithm ensures a mix of content types and genres that align with the user's interests, providing a balanced viewing experience.

Dynamic Personalization

Recommendations are continuously updated based on real-time data. As users interact with new content, their profiles are refined, and suggestions are adjusted accordingly.

The role of demographic and geographic data

Demographic and geographic data enhance personalization by providing additional layers of context:

Localization

Recommendations are tailored to match the user's geographic location, offering content in their preferred language and relevant to their region.

Cultural Preferences

Understanding cultural nuances helps the algorithm recommend content that resonates with the user's cultural background and interests.

Demographic Trends

Age, gender, and other demographic factors influence content preferences, allowing the algorithm to suggest videos that appeal to specific demographic groups.

2.3 Continuous Learning and Adaptation

How YouTube algorithms learn from new data

YouTube's algorithms are designed to continuously learn and adapt based on new data. This process involves:

Real-Time Data Processing

The algorithms process vast amounts of data in real-time, analyzing user interactions as they occur to update recommendations dynamically.

Feedback Integration

User feedback, such as likes, dislikes, and watch history, is integrated into the learning process, helping the algorithms adjust to changing preferences.

Adaptive Models

Machine learning models are regularly retrained on new data, allowing them to adapt to emerging trends and shifting user behaviors.

The process of updating recommendations in real-time

Updating recommendations in real-time involves several key steps:

Data Collection

Continuous data collection from user interactions, including watch history, search queries, and engagement metrics.

Model Updating

Machine learning models are updated with the latest data, refining their predictions and improving accuracy.

Recommendation Adjustment

The updated models adjust recommendations based on the most recent user data, ensuring that suggestions remain relevant and timely.

Handling changes in user behavior and trends

The ability to handle changes in user behavior and trends is crucial for maintaining the relevance of recommendations:

Trend Analysis

Algorithms monitor trending content and shifts in user preferences, adapting recommendations to reflect current interests.

User Behavior Tracking

Changes in individual user behavior, such as new interests or shifts in viewing patterns, are tracked and integrated into the recommendation process.

A/B Testing and Experimentation

YouTube conducts A/B testing and experiments to evaluate the effectiveness of different recommendation strategies, allowing for continuous improvement.

By leveraging these techniques, YouTube's algorithms ensure that recommendations are always aligned with user preferences, providing a personalized and engaging viewing experience.

Chapter 3
Search Algorithms

3.1 Understanding YouTube Search

The components of YouTube's search engine

YouTube's search engine is a complex system designed to help users find videos that match their queries. It comprises several key components:

Crawlers and Indexers

These are automated bots that crawl YouTube's vast database of videos, extracting information such as titles, descriptions, tags, and transcripts. This data is then indexed to make it searchable.

Search Query Processor

When a user enters a search query, the query processor interprets the input, breaking it down into keywords and phrases that can be matched against the indexed data.

Ranking Algorithms

These algorithms determine the order in which search results are displayed. They take into account a variety of factors, including relevance, popularity, user engagement, and freshness of the content.

User Interface

The user interface presents the search results in an organized and accessible manner, typically displaying a mix of videos, channels, playlists, and other relevant content.

How search results are ranked and displayed

Search results on YouTube are ranked and displayed based on a combination of factors designed to ensure relevance and user satisfaction:

Relevance

The primary factor is how well a video matches the search query. This involves analyzing the keywords in the title, description, tags, and transcripts.

Engagement Metrics

Videos with higher engagement—measured through likes, comments, shares, and watch time—are likely to rank higher as they indicate quality and user interest.

Freshness

Newer videos may be prioritized, especially for queries related to current events or trending topics, ensuring that users receive the most up-to-date information.

Watch Time

Videos that keep viewers engaged for longer periods are favored as they contribute to overall user satisfaction and platform retention.

Channel Authority

Channels with a history of producing high-quality, relevant content may receive a boost in search rankings.

The difference between organic and paid search results

YouTube search results can include both organic and paid listings:

Organic Search Results

These are the unpaid search results that YouTube's algorithms determine to be the most relevant to a user's query. They are ranked based on relevance, engagement metrics, and other factors mentioned above.

Paid Search Results (Ads)

These results are advertisements that appear at the top of the search results page. Advertisers bid on keywords to have their videos featured prominently. While marked as ads, they still need to be relevant to the search query to ensure user satisfaction.

3.2 Keyword Optimization and Metadata

The importance of keywords in titles, descriptions, and tags

Keywords are critical for improving the visibility of videos in search results. They help YouTube's search engine understand the content of the video and match it with user queries.

Titles

Including relevant keywords in the video title helps YouTube quickly identify the video's subject matter. A well-crafted title with primary keywords can significantly boost search ranking.

Descriptions

The video description provides more context and allows for the inclusion of additional keywords. Detailed descriptions help improve search visibility and can include links, timestamps, and supplementary information.

Tags

Tags are keywords that help YouTube categorize the video content. Including a mix of broad and specific tags can enhance discoverability by associating the video with related content and search terms.

Best practices for metadata optimization

Effective metadata optimization involves several best practices:

Keyword Research

Conducting keyword research to identify popular and relevant search terms related to the video content is essential. Tools like Google Trends, YouTube's autocomplete feature, and keyword research tools can be valuable resources.

Clear and Descriptive Titles

Crafting clear and descriptive titles that include primary keywords while remaining engaging and click-worthy.

Detailed Descriptions

Writing comprehensive video descriptions that include keywords naturally, provide valuable information, and encourage viewer engagement with calls to action.

Relevant Tags

Using a mix of broad and specific tags that accurately reflect the video content. Avoid keyword stuffing, as it can negatively impact search rankings.

Accurate Transcripts

Providing accurate video transcripts can enhance searchability, especially for videos with spoken content. Transcripts can be used to capture additional keywords and improve accessibility.

The impact of video transcripts on searchability

Video transcripts play a significant role in enhancing searchability:

Keyword Inclusion

Transcripts allow for the inclusion of additional keywords that may not fit naturally in titles, descriptions, or tags. This helps improve the video's relevance to various search queries.

Accessibility

Transcripts make content accessible to a wider audience, including those who are deaf or hard of hearing. Improved accessibility can lead to higher engagement and better search rankings.

Content Understanding

Transcripts provide YouTube's algorithms with a detailed understanding of the video content, allowing for more accurate indexing and search matching.

3.3 User Intent and Contextual Relevance

Analyzing user intent behind search queries

Understanding user intent is crucial for delivering relevant search results. User intent can be categorized into several types:

Informational Intent

Users seeking information or answers to specific questions. Videos that provide clear and concise information are prioritized.

Navigational Intent

Users looking to find a specific video, channel, or playlist. Search results are tailored to help users quickly locate the desired content.

Transactional Intent

Users interested in making a purchase or engaging in a specific action, such as downloading or subscribing. Videos related to product reviews, unboxings, or how-to guides are favored.

Entertainment Intent

Users looking for entertainment or leisure content. Recommendations focus on popular and engaging videos within the user's areas of interest.

The role of context in delivering relevant results

Context plays a vital role in delivering relevant search results. Factors influencing contextual relevance include:

User History

Past interactions, watch history, and search behavior provide context for current queries, allowing the algorithm to tailor results to individual preferences.

Location

Geographic location can influence search results, especially for queries related to local events, services, or news.

Device and Time of Day

The type of device used (e.g., mobile, desktop) and the time of day can affect search results. For example, mobile users might see shorter, more digestible content, while desktop users might get longer, more detailed videos.

Current Trends

Trending topics and current events can influence search results, ensuring that timely and relevant content is prioritized.

How search algorithms handle ambiguous or vague queries

Handling ambiguous or vague queries involves several strategies:

Query Expansion

The algorithm may expand the query to include related terms and synonyms, providing a broader range of results that might match the user's intent.

User Behavior Analysis

Analyzing previous search behavior and watch history helps disambiguate vague queries. If a user frequently searches for cooking videos, a query like "recipes" might prioritize cooking-related content.

Search Suggestions

Offering search suggestions based on partial queries or common search patterns helps users refine their queries and find relevant content.

Contextual Clues

Utilizing contextual clues from the user's current session, such as recent searches or watched videos, helps tailor results to the user's likely intent.

By leveraging these techniques, YouTube's search algorithms aim to provide accurate and relevant search results, enhancing user satisfaction and engagement with the platform.

Chapter 4

Engagement Metrics and Ranking

4.1 Key Engagement Metrics

Definitions and examples of engagement metrics

Engagement metrics are quantitative measures that reflect how users interact with videos on YouTube. Key engagement metrics include:

Views

Definition: The number of times a video has been watched.

Example: A video with 10,000 views has been played 10,000 times by different or the same users.

Likes and Dislikes

Definition: The number of thumbs-up (likes) and thumbs-down (dislikes) a video receives.

Example: A video with 2,000 likes and 100 dislikes shows a positive reception from the audience.

Comments

Definition: Text responses from viewers, ranging from feedback to discussions.

Example: A video with 500 comments may indicate active viewer engagement and interest.

Shares

Definition: The number of times a video is shared on social media or other platforms.

Example: A video shared 300 times on Facebook suggests its content is valued and worth spreading.

How engagement metrics influence video ranking

Engagement metrics significantly influence how YouTube ranks videos, impacting their visibility in search results and recommendations:

Views

High view counts suggest popularity and relevance, boosting a video's ranking.

Likes and Dislikes

A higher ratio of likes to dislikes indicates positive reception, helping improve ranking. Dislikes can signal content quality issues but are also considered for balance.

Comments

A high volume of comments signifies viewer interaction and interest, enhancing a video's ranking due to perceived engagement.

Shares

Videos that are frequently shared indicate content value and broader reach, positively affecting ranking.

The interplay between different types of engagement

Different types of engagement metrics interplay to form a holistic picture of a video's performance:

Views and Watch Time

While high view counts are important, longer watch times indicate deeper engagement, making both crucial for ranking.

Likes, Dislikes, and Comments

Likes and positive comments boost rankings, but dislikes and negative comments can provide valuable feedback for algorithm adjustments.

Shares and External Traffic

Shared videos drive external traffic, increasing views and potentially boosting watch time, enhancing overall engagement metrics.

4.2 Watch Time and Session Duration

The significance of watch time in algorithm decisions

Watch time, the total amount of time viewers spend watching a video, is a critical metric for YouTube's algorithms:

Viewer Engagement

Longer watch times indicate that viewers find the content engaging and valuable, leading to higher rankings.

Ad Revenue

Extended watch times increase ad exposure, contributing to YouTube's revenue, making watch time a key focus.

User Satisfaction

High watch times correlate with user satisfaction, encouraging the algorithm to promote such content to enhance the viewer experience.

Strategies to increase watch time and session duration

To maximize watch time and session duration, content creators can employ several strategies:

Engaging Introductions

Captivating introductions grab viewer attention and encourage them to watch the entire video.

Consistent Quality

Maintaining high content quality throughout the video keeps viewers engaged and reduces drop-off rates.

Calls to Action

Encouraging viewers to watch more videos, subscribe, or explore playlists can extend session duration.

End Screens and Playlists

Using end screens to promote related videos and organizing content into playlists helps retain viewers on the channel.

The relationship between watch time and viewer retention

Watch time and viewer retention are closely linked:

Viewer Retention

High viewer retention means viewers are watching a significant portion of the video, contributing to longer watch times.

Algorithmic Favorability

Videos with high retention rates signal to YouTube that the content is valuable, leading to higher rankings and more recommendations.

Content Strategies

Creating engaging, well-paced content with minimal filler helps maintain high retention and watch times.

4.3 User Interaction Signals

Analyzing the impact of likes, dislikes, and comments

User interaction signals, including likes, dislikes, and comments, provide valuable insights into content performance:

Likes and Dislikes

Positive Impact: High likes and low dislikes indicate content approval, boosting video ranking.

Negative Impact: High dislikes can lower ranking but also offer constructive feedback for creators.

Comments

Positive Impact: A high volume of positive comments reflects active engagement and interest, improving ranking.

Negative Impact: Negative comments provide feedback but can also detract from viewer perception if not addressed.

The role of click-through rate (CTR) in ranking

CTR, the percentage of users who click on a video after seeing its thumbnail, is a crucial metric for ranking:

Thumbnail and Title Optimization

Engaging thumbnails and titles increase CTR, signaling to the algorithm that the video is attracting viewer interest.

Search and Discovery

High CTR in search results and recommendations suggests relevance and value, leading to higher rankings.

Content Relevance

A high CTR, combined with long watch times, indicates that the video content meets viewer expectations, reinforcing its ranking.

How user feedback shapes algorithmic responses

User feedback, through interactions and engagement metrics, shapes how algorithms respond to and promote content:

Dynamic Adjustments

The algorithm continuously adjusts rankings based on real-time feedback from user interactions.

Personalized Recommendations

Feedback influences personalized recommendations, ensuring viewers receive content aligned with their preferences.

Content Quality Improvement

Analyzing user feedback helps content creators improve quality, enhancing future performance and engagement.

By understanding and leveraging engagement metrics, watch time, and user interaction signals, content creators can optimize their videos for better visibility, higher rankings, and sustained viewer engagement on YouTube.

Chapter 5
Content Quality and
Creator Reputation

5.1 Assessing Content Quality

Criteria used by algorithms to evaluate content quality

YouTube algorithms assess content quality using a variety of criteria to ensure viewers receive valuable and engaging content. Key criteria include:

Viewer Engagement

High engagement metrics, such as views, likes, comments, shares, and watch time, indicate that content resonates with viewers.

Audience Retention

Videos with higher retention rates, where viewers watch a substantial portion of the content, are considered high-quality.

Production Value

Clear audio, high-definition video, good lighting, and professional editing enhance perceived quality.

Relevance and Information

Videos that provide accurate, comprehensive, and relevant information or entertainment are favored.

Thumbnail and Title Accuracy

Thumbnails and titles that accurately represent the video content contribute to a positive viewer experience and are part of quality assessment.

User Feedback

Positive feedback through likes, shares, and comments, as well as minimal dislikes, indicates quality content.

The importance of production value and viewer satisfaction

Production value and viewer satisfaction are crucial for content success on YouTube:

Production Value

High production value makes videos more professional and enjoyable to watch, encouraging longer viewing times and repeated visits.

Investing in good equipment and editing software can significantly improve production quality.

Viewer Satisfaction

Satisfied viewers are more likely to engage with the content, subscribe to the channel, and recommend videos to others.

Positive viewer experiences lead to higher engagement metrics, which boost algorithmic favorability.

Balancing quality with quantity in content creation

Finding the right balance between quality and quantity is essential for sustained success on YouTube:

Quality over Quantity

While frequent uploads can keep the audience engaged, consistently high-quality content is more important for long-term success.

High-quality videos are more likely to attract and retain viewers, leading to better performance metrics.

Regular Upload Schedule

Establishing a consistent upload schedule helps build viewer expectations and maintain engagement.

Balancing production time to ensure both quality and regular uploads is key.

Content Planning

Planning content in advance allows creators to maintain a steady flow of quality videos without compromising production value.

Creating a mix of in-depth, high-production videos and quicker, lighter content can help maintain consistency.

5.2 Building Creator Reputation

How algorithms track and evaluate creator history

YouTube algorithms track a creator's history to evaluate reputation and reliability:

Consistency

Regular uploads and consistent content quality signal reliability and dedication, which are valued by the algorithm.

Engagement Metrics

Historical engagement metrics, such as views, watch time, likes, comments, and shares, contribute to a creator's reputation.

Compliance with Guidelines

Adherence to YouTube's community guidelines and policies is critical. Violations can negatively impact a creator's reputation.

Viewer Feedback

Positive viewer feedback over time indicates a reputable creator who consistently delivers valuable content.

The impact of consistency and niche focus

Consistency and niche focus are key factors in building a strong creator reputation:

Consistency

Regular uploads help maintain audience interest and engagement, which are crucial for building a loyal viewer base.

Consistency in content style, tone, and quality reinforces brand identity and trust.

Niche Focus

Focusing on a specific niche allows creators to become experts in their field, attracting a dedicated audience.

Niche content can lead to higher engagement rates as it caters to a targeted audience interested in specific topics.

Strategies for building a strong creator reputation

Creators can implement various strategies to build and maintain a strong reputation:

Content Quality

Prioritize high-quality production and valuable content to enhance viewer satisfaction and engagement.

Engagement

Actively engage with viewers through comments, community posts, and social media to build a loyal community.

Consistency

Maintain a regular upload schedule and ensure consistent content quality to build trust and reliability.

Adherence to Guidelines

Follow YouTube's community guidelines and policies to avoid violations that can harm reputation and ranking.

Branding

Develop a strong brand identity through consistent visuals, tone, and messaging to make content easily recognizable.

5.3 Handling Content Violations and Demonetization

The role of community guidelines and policies

YouTube's community guidelines and policies are designed to maintain a safe and respectful environment for all users:

Content Standards

Guidelines outline acceptable content, covering areas such as hate speech, violence, nudity, and harmful or dangerous acts.

Ad Policies

Ad policies specify content suitability for monetization, ensuring ads are placed on videos that meet advertiser-friendly standards.

Enforcement

YouTube uses automated systems and human reviewers to enforce guidelines and take action against violations.

How algorithmic moderation works

Algorithmic moderation involves automated systems that scan content for potential violations:

Content Scanning

Algorithms analyze video titles, descriptions, tags, thumbnails, and audio/visual elements for guideline violations.

Flagging and Review

Potentially violating content is flagged for further review, often involving human moderators for final decisions.

Automated Actions

The system can take immediate actions, such as removing videos, issuing strikes, or disabling monetization for violations.

Consequences of content violations on ranking and monetization

Content violations can have severe consequences for ranking and monetization:

Ranking Impact

Violations can lead to reduced visibility in search results and recommendations, impacting overall video performance.

Demonetization

Videos found to violate ad policies may lose their monetization status, significantly affecting revenue.

Channel Strikes

Repeated violations can result in strikes against the channel, leading to restrictions, suspension, or termination.

Reputation Damage

Violations can harm a creator's reputation, making it difficult to rebuild trust and regain lost viewers.

By understanding how algorithms assess content quality and creator reputation, and by adhering to community guidelines, creators can optimize their content for better visibility, engagement, and sustained success on YouTube.

Chapter 6
Audience
Development and Growth

6.1 Audience Retention Strategies

Techniques for retaining viewers throughout a video

Retaining viewers throughout a video is crucial for increasing watch time and improving engagement metrics, which are highly valued by YouTube's algorithm. Here are some effective techniques:

Hook Viewers Early

Engaging Introductions: Capture attention within the first few seconds with compelling hooks, such as a surprising fact, a question, or an intriguing preview of what's to come.

Clear Value Proposition: Clearly communicate the video's value and what viewers can expect to gain by watching.

Structured Content

Logical Flow: Organize content in a logical sequence to keep viewers following along effortlessly.

Visual and Auditory Cues: Use on-screen text, graphics, and audio cues to emphasize key points and guide viewers through the video.

Storytelling

Narrative Techniques: Use storytelling elements to make the content more engaging and relatable.

Emotional Connection: Connect with viewers on an emotional level through personal anecdotes or impactful stories.

Engagement Prompts

Call to Actions (CTAs): Include CTAs to encourage viewers to like, comment, and subscribe.

Interactive Elements: Use polls, questions, and prompts to engage viewers actively.

The importance of engaging introductions and content pacing

Engaging introductions and well-paced content are vital for maintaining viewer interest and retention:

Engaging Introductions

First Impressions: The introduction sets the tone for the rest of the video. A strong start helps to hook viewers immediately.

Preview Content: Briefly preview what the video will cover to create anticipation and curiosity.

Content Pacing

Avoid Monotony: Vary the pacing by mixing up visuals, changing scenes, and including different types of content (e.g., interviews, B-roll footage).

Keep It Moving: Maintain a steady pace that keeps viewers engaged without overwhelming them.

Transitional Elements: Use transitions and chapter markers to break up the content and make it easier to digest.

Analyzing audience retention graphs for insights

Audience retention graphs provide valuable insights into viewer behavior and preferences:

Identifying Drop-off Points

Sharp Declines: Look for points where a significant number of viewers stop watching. Analyze what happened at those moments (e.g., boring segments, irrelevant content).

Gradual Declines: Identify trends in gradual drop-offs to understand overall pacing issues.

High Retention Segments

Popular Sections: Determine which parts of the video had the highest retention and try to replicate those elements in future content.

Average View Duration

Benchmarking: Compare the average view duration against the total video length to gauge overall performance.

Improvement Areas: Use retention data to continuously refine content strategy and improve viewer retention.

6.2 Subscriber Growth and Engagement

Factors influencing subscriber growth

Several factors contribute to subscriber growth on YouTube:

Consistent Content

Regular Uploads: Maintain a consistent upload schedule to keep your audience engaged and coming back for more.

Quality and Relevance: Ensure that content is consistently high-quality and relevant to your target audience.

Value Proposition

Unique Selling Point (USP): Clearly communicate what makes your channel unique and why viewers should subscribe.

Content Variety: Offer a variety of content types (e.g., tutorials, vlogs, reviews) to appeal to a broader audience.

Engagement

Interaction: Engage with viewers through comments, community posts, and social media to build a loyal following.

Personal Connection: Establish a personal connection with viewers by sharing behind-the-scenes content and personal stories.

Strategies for converting viewers into subscribers

Converting viewers into subscribers requires strategic efforts:

Compelling CTAs

Direct Requests: Ask viewers to subscribe at natural points in the video, such as the beginning, middle, and end.

Benefits Highlight: Explain the benefits of subscribing, such as exclusive content, updates, and community engagement.

Content Teasers

Future Content: Tease upcoming videos to create anticipation and encourage viewers to subscribe for updates.

Series and Playlists: Create series and playlists that encourage viewers to subscribe for continuity.

Subscription Incentives

Giveaways and Contests: Offer incentives like giveaways and contests to encourage subscriptions.

Exclusive Content: Provide exclusive content or early access to subscribers to add value.

Engaging subscribers through notifications and community posts

Engaging subscribers helps maintain their interest and encourages loyalty:

Notifications

Enable Bell Icon: Encourage subscribers to click the bell icon to receive notifications about new uploads.

Timely Updates: Notify subscribers about new content, live streams, and important updates through YouTube notifications.

Community Posts

Interactive Content: Use community posts to share polls, questions, and updates to engage with your audience.

Behind-the-Scenes: Share behind-the-scenes content, sneak peeks, and personal updates to build a stronger connection with subscribers.

6.3 Community Building and Interaction

The role of community engagement in algorithm

favorability

Community engagement plays a significant role in enhancing algorithm favorability:

Increased Engagement

Comments and Interactions: High levels of comments and interactions signal to the algorithm that the content is engaging and valuable.

Shares and Likes: Increased shares and likes indicate content popularity and can improve visibility.

Loyal Audience

Retention and Repeat Views: A loyal audience that regularly watches and engages with content boosts retention rates and overall engagement metrics.

Best practices for fostering a loyal audience

Building a loyal audience requires consistent effort and strategic practices:

Authenticity and Transparency

Personal Connection: Be authentic and transparent with your audience to build trust and loyalty.

Open Communication: Engage in open communication, respond to comments, and address viewer feedback.

Value and Consistency

Consistent Quality: Provide consistent value through high-quality content.

Regular Engagement: Engage with your audience regularly through comments, community posts, and live interactions.

Community Initiatives

Collaborations: Collaborate with other creators to introduce your audience to new content and build a broader community.

Events and Challenges: Host events, challenges, and interactive sessions to foster community participation.

Leveraging community features like comments, polls, and live streams

Utilizing community features effectively enhances audience interaction and loyalty:

Comments

Active Moderation: Actively moderate comments to foster a positive and respectful community.

Engagement: Respond to comments, ask questions, and encourage discussions to increase interaction.

Polls

Audience Feedback: Use polls to gather audience feedback and involve them in content decisions.

Engagement Boost: Polls can increase engagement by encouraging viewers to participate and share their opinions.

Live Streams

Real-Time Interaction: Host live streams to interact with your audience in real-time, answer questions, and discuss topics of interest.

Exclusive Content: Offer exclusive content or behind-the-scenes insights during live streams to incentivize participation.

By implementing effective audience retention strategies, focusing on subscriber growth and engagement, and building a strong community, creators can significantly enhance their channel's performance and foster sustained growth on YouTube.

Chapter 7
Algorithmic Impact on Video Promotion

7.1 Trends and Virality

How algorithms detect and promote trending content

YouTube algorithms are designed to identify and promote trending content through a variety of mechanisms:

Rapid Engagement

High Engagement Rates: Algorithms detect videos with high engagement rates, such as views, likes, comments, and shares, especially within a short time after upload.

Viewer Retention: High viewer retention rates indicate that viewers are staying engaged with the content, which is a key factor in promoting videos.

Social Signals

Shares on Social Media: Videos shared widely on social media platforms can trigger the algorithm to recognize them as trending.

Mentions and Links: Videos that are frequently mentioned or linked to on other websites or in blogs can also gain algorithmic attention.

Search and Discovery

Increased Search Volume: Spikes in search queries related to a video or its topics can signal trending potential.

Discovery Features: Being featured in YouTube's discovery sections, such as the "Trending" tab, is both a result and a further enhancer of trend detection.

The characteristics of viral videos

Viral videos typically share certain characteristics that make them highly shareable and engaging:

Emotional Appeal

Strong Emotions: Videos that evoke strong emotions, whether it's humor, awe, sadness, or inspiration, tend to be shared more widely.

Relatability: Content that viewers can relate to on a personal level often goes viral.

Shareability

Easy to Share: Videos that are short, concise, and easy to understand are more likely to be shared.

Social Relevance: Content that aligns with current events, popular culture, or trending topics is more likely to be shared.

Quality and Production

High Production Value: Well-produced videos with clear audio, good lighting, and professional editing stand out.

Engaging Thumbnails and Titles: Eye-catching thumbnails and intriguing titles can significantly boost click-through rates.

Strategies for creating trend-worthy content

Creating content that has the potential to trend involves a combination of creativity, timing, and understanding your audience:

Timely Content

Current Events: Create content that ties into current events, trends, or popular culture.

Seasonal Themes: Leverage holidays, seasons, and annual events to create timely and relevant content.

Engaging Formats

Challenges and Series: Create challenge videos or content series that encourage viewer participation and repeated viewing.

Collaborations: Partner with other creators to tap into their audience and increase your content's reach.

Audience Insights

Analyze Trends: Use tools like Google Trends and YouTube Analytics to understand what topics are currently popular.

Feedback Loop: Pay attention to viewer feedback and adapt your content to meet their interests and preferences.

7.2 Cross-Promotions and Collaborations

The impact of cross-promotions on algorithmic ranking

Cross-promotions and collaborations can significantly boost algorithmic ranking by increasing engagement and visibility:

Increased Reach

Audience Overlap: Collaborations allow creators to tap into each other's audiences, increasing reach and potential engagement.

Diverse Engagement: Cross-promotions can introduce your content to new viewer demographics, enhancing overall engagement.

Engagement Boost

Shared Interest: When creators with similar or complementary content collaborate, it tends to boost engagement from viewers interested in both channels.

Interactivity: Collaborative videos often include interactive elements that encourage viewers to engage more deeply.

Best practices for effective collaborations

To maximize the impact of collaborations, consider these best practices:

Aligned Goals

Shared Objectives: Ensure that both parties have aligned goals and clear expectations for the collaboration.

Mutual Benefit: Choose collaborators whose audience and content style align well with yours for mutual benefit.

Clear Communication

Planning and Coordination: Plan the collaboration thoroughly, including content creation, promotion, and engagement strategies.

Roles and Responsibilities: Clearly define roles and responsibilities to ensure a smooth collaboration process.

Promotion and Follow-up

Cross-Promote: Promote the collaborative content on both channels and across social media platforms.

Engage with Viewers: Follow up with viewers by engaging in comments and encouraging them to check out the collaborator's channel.

Leveraging network effects to boost visibility

Network effects can amplify the visibility of your content through strategic collaborations and promotions:

Chain Reactions

Viral Loop: Each new viewer can potentially share the video with their network, creating a chain reaction that amplifies visibility.

Content Ecosystem: Collaborations can create a content ecosystem where viewers move between related channels, increasing overall engagement.

Cumulative Growth

Snowball Effect: As more viewers engage with and share the content, the algorithm is more likely to promote it further, leading to exponential growth.

Sustained Engagement: Regular collaborations can keep the momentum going, sustaining long-term engagement and growth.

7.3 Paid Promotions and Advertisements

Understanding YouTube's ad algorithms

YouTube's ad algorithms are designed to serve relevant ads to the right audience, optimizing both advertiser goals and user experience:

Targeting Mechanisms

Demographic Targeting: Ads are targeted based on user demographics such as age, gender, and location.

Behavioral Targeting: User behavior, including watch history, search queries, and engagement patterns, informs ad targeting.

Relevance and Quality

Ad Quality Score: Ads are evaluated based on their relevance, engagement, and user feedback.

Bidding System: Advertisers bid for ad placements, and higher bids for high-quality, relevant ads are more likely to win placements.

The role of paid promotions in organic ranking

Paid promotions can have a significant impact on organic ranking by increasing visibility and engagement:

Initial Boost

Increased Views: Paid promotions can lead to a rapid increase in views, which can trigger the algorithm to promote the video organically.

Higher Engagement: Ads that lead to high engagement (likes, comments, shares) can further enhance organic visibility.

Algorithmic Favorability

Watch Time: Ads that result in longer watch times can positively influence the video's ranking.

Subscriber Growth: Paid promotions that convert viewers into subscribers can improve the overall performance of the channel.

Balancing paid and organic growth strategies

A balanced approach to paid and organic growth can maximize long-term success on YouTube:

Integrated Campaigns

Complementary Strategies: Use paid promotions to complement organic growth strategies, ensuring a cohesive approach.

Targeted Ads: Focus paid promotions on specific goals, such as launching new content or reaching new audiences, while maintaining organic content efforts.

ROI Analysis

Measure Effectiveness: Regularly analyze the return on investment (ROI) of paid promotions to ensure they are delivering the desired outcomes.

Adjust Strategies: Continuously adjust both paid and organic strategies based on performance data and audience feedback.

Sustainable Growth

Long-term Focus: Aim for sustainable growth by building a loyal audience through consistent, high-quality content while using paid promotions to accelerate growth.

Audience Engagement: Prioritize engaging with your audience to foster loyalty and long-term retention, balancing immediate visibility with lasting connections.

By understanding how algorithms detect and promote trending content, leveraging cross-promotions and collaborations, and effectively using paid promotions, creators can significantly enhance their video promotion efforts and achieve sustained growth on YouTube.

Chapter 8
Algorithm
Transparency and Criticism

8.1 Transparency Efforts by YouTube

Initiatives to increase algorithm transparency

YouTube has undertaken several initiatives to enhance transparency around how its algorithms function:

Creator Updates

YouTube Creator Blog: Regular posts explaining new features, algorithm updates, and best practices for creators.

Community Guidelines Updates: Clear and accessible updates to community guidelines, helping creators understand what content is permissible.

Educational Resources

YouTube Creators Academy: Online courses and resources that provide in-depth information on how the platform works, including algorithmic insights.

Algorithm Insights Videos: Official YouTube videos featuring team members explaining how different parts of the algorithm operate.

Algorithm Research and Reports

Transparency Reports: Periodic reports that detail how policies are enforced and provide data on content removals, strikes, and appeals.

Collaborations with Researchers: Partnerships with academic institutions and independent researchers to study and publish findings on algorithmic impacts.

How YouTube communicates changes and updates to creators

YouTube employs multiple channels to ensure that creators are informed about changes and updates to algorithms:

Notifications

Direct Notifications: Important updates are often communicated directly through notifications in the YouTube Studio dashboard.

Email Alerts: Critical changes and new features are also communicated via email to ensure creators are aware and can adapt accordingly.

Community Posts and Forums

YouTube Community Tab: Updates and insights are shared on the Community Tab, allowing for direct engagement with the creator community.

YouTube Help Forum: An official forum where creators can ask questions, share concerns, and get official responses from YouTube representatives.

Creator Events

YouTube Creator Summits: Annual events that bring together top creators to discuss platform changes, share feedback, and learn about upcoming features.

Webinars and Live Q&A: Regular online sessions where YouTube staff explain new updates and answer questions from the community.

The importance of transparency for trust and accountability

Transparency in algorithmic processes is crucial for maintaining trust and accountability between YouTube and its user base:

Building Trust

Clear Communication: When YouTube clearly communicates how algorithms work and why changes are made, it helps build trust with creators and viewers.

Predictability: Understanding algorithmic rules and updates helps creators predict and adapt to changes, reducing frustration and uncertainty.

Accountability

Responsibility: Transparency holds YouTube accountable for the impacts of its algorithms on the creator community and the broader public.

Feedback Loops: Open communication channels allow creators to provide feedback, helping YouTube refine and improve its algorithms over time.

8.2 Common Criticisms of YouTube Algorithms

Issues related to bias, misinformation, and content diversity

YouTube's algorithms have faced several criticisms regarding their impact on content and user experience:

Algorithmic Bias

Echo Chambers: Algorithms that prioritize similar content can create echo chambers, reinforcing users' existing beliefs and reducing exposure to diverse perspectives.

Representation: Bias in algorithms can lead to underrepresentation of minority voices and content, impacting content diversity on the platform.

Misinformation

Spread of False Information: Algorithms that prioritize engagement can inadvertently promote sensationalist and misleading content, contributing to the spread of misinformation.

Fact-Checking: The effectiveness of YouTube's measures to combat misinformation, such as fact-check labels and authoritative sources, remains a subject of ongoing debate.

Content Diversity

Homogenization: The focus on popular and high-engagement content can lead to a homogenization of content, where niche or alternative perspectives struggle to gain visibility.

Discovery Challenges: Smaller or newer creators often find it challenging to get their content discovered amidst the dominance of well-established channels.

The impact of algorithmic changes on creators and viewers

Algorithmic changes can have significant and sometimes controversial impacts on both creators and viewers:

Creators

Monetization Shifts: Changes to algorithms that impact how videos are recommended or demonetized can significantly affect a creator's revenue and livelihood.

Content Strategy: Creators often need to constantly adapt their content strategy to align with algorithmic updates, which can be resource-intensive and stressful.

Viewers

Content Consumption: Algorithmic changes can alter the type of content that viewers are exposed to, impacting their overall viewing experience.

Filter Bubbles: Viewers may find themselves in filter bubbles where they are exposed to a narrow range of content, limiting their exposure to diverse viewpoints.

Case studies of controversial algorithm decisions

Examining specific instances where YouTube's algorithmic decisions have sparked controversy:

Adpocalypse (2017)

Overview: Major advertisers pulled their ads from YouTube due to concerns over their ads appearing alongside inappropriate content. YouTube responded by tightening its ad policies, which resulted in many creators experiencing significant drops in ad revenue.

Impact: This led to widespread criticism from creators who felt unfairly penalized, and sparked debates over the balance between advertiser demands and creator freedom.

Recommendation Algorithm Adjustments (2019)

Overview: YouTube announced changes to its recommendation system to reduce the spread of borderline content and misinformation. This included adjustments to downrank conspiracy theories and harmful content.

Impact: While intended to improve content quality, some creators argued that these changes disproportionately affected their visibility and reach, especially those in the commentary and independent news sectors.

COPPA Compliance (2020)

Overview: In response to regulatory pressures under the Children's Online Privacy Protection Act (COPPA), YouTube made significant changes to how it handles content made for children. This included restricting data collection and disabling certain features on kids' videos.

Impact: Many family and kids content creators faced reduced engagement and revenue, leading to calls for more nuanced and creator-friendly policy implementations.

8.3 Balancing Algorithmic Decisions

The challenge of balancing diverse stakeholder interests

YouTube faces the complex challenge of balancing the needs and interests of various stakeholders, including:

Creators

Monetization and Visibility: Creators seek fair monetization opportunities and visibility for their content.

Creative Freedom: Maintaining creative freedom while adhering to platform policies and guidelines.

Advertisers

Brand Safety: Ensuring ads appear alongside appropriate and brand-safe content.

Engagement and ROI: Maximizing ad effectiveness and return on investment.

Viewers

Content Quality and Relevance: Delivering high-quality, relevant content that enhances user experience.

Diverse Perspectives: Providing exposure to a broad range of viewpoints and content types.

Approaches to mitigate negative impacts

To address the potential negative impacts of algorithmic decisions, YouTube can employ several strategies:

Algorithmic Fairness

Bias Mitigation: Implementing measures to detect and mitigate biases in algorithms, ensuring fair treatment of all creators and content types.

Diversity and Inclusion: Actively promoting diverse voices and content to ensure a wide range of perspectives are represented.

User and Creator Feedback

Feedback Mechanisms: Providing robust feedback mechanisms for creators and viewers to voice their concerns and suggestions.

Iterative Improvements: Continuously refining algorithms based on feedback and data-driven insights to address emerging issues.

Transparency and Communication

Clear Communication: Transparently communicating the rationale behind algorithmic changes and their expected impact.

Educational Resources: Offering resources and guidance to help creators understand and adapt to algorithmic updates.

The role of human oversight in algorithmic decisions

While algorithms play a critical role in content curation and recommendation, human oversight remains essential:

Human Moderation

Content Review: Employing human moderators to review flagged content and ensure adherence to community guidelines.

Dispute Resolution: Providing a process for creators to appeal algorithmic decisions and have their content reviewed by human moderators.

Ethical Considerations

Ethical Review: Integrating ethical considerations into algorithm development and deployment to prevent harmful outcomes.

Stakeholder Engagement: Engaging with diverse stakeholders, including creators, viewers, advertisers, and external experts, to ensure balanced and ethical algorithmic practices.

Continuous Improvement

Algorithm Audits: Conducting regular audits of algorithms to identify and address potential biases and unintended consequences.

Adaptive Learning: Ensuring algorithms continuously learn and adapt based on new data, feedback, and emerging trends, guided by human oversight.

By increasing transparency, addressing common criticisms, and balancing algorithmic decisions with human oversight, YouTube can create a more fair, inclusive, and accountable platform for all its stakeholders.

Chapter 9
Future of YouTube Algorithms

9.1 Emerging Technologies in Algorithm Development

The Role of AI and Machine Learning Advancements

Artificial intelligence (AI) and machine learning (ML) are at the forefront of YouTube's algorithmic evolution. These technologies are becoming more sophisticated, allowing YouTube to deliver more accurate and personalized content recommendations.

1: Deep Learning Models

Neural Networks: Utilization of complex neural networks to process vast amounts of data and identify patterns that inform content recommendations.

Natural Language Processing (NLP): Enhancements in NLP help algorithms better understand video content, titles, descriptions, and comments to improve search accuracy and recommendations.

2: Reinforcement Learning

Adaptive Algorithms: Algorithms that use reinforcement learning can adapt based on user interactions, learning what content maximizes engagement and satisfaction.

Personalized Learning: These models continuously learn and refine their predictions, providing increasingly tailored content to individual users.

3: Collaborative Filtering

User-Based Filtering: Recommendations based on similarities between users' viewing histories.

Item-Based Filtering: Suggestions derived from similarities between content items, helping users discover new videos similar to those they've liked.

Predictive Analytics and Its Future Impact

Predictive analytics leverages historical data to forecast future behaviors and trends, significantly impacting how YouTube algorithms function.

1: Viewer Behavior Prediction

Engagement Trends: Algorithms predict which videos are likely to be trending or go viral based on early user interactions.

Retention Analysis: Identifying factors that contribute to longer watch times and optimizing recommendations accordingly.

2: Content Performance Forecasting

Success Prediction: Algorithms forecast the potential success of new uploads based on creator history, content type, and initial viewer response.

Trend Analysis: Identifying emerging trends and suggesting content topics that align with user interests.

Integration of Augmented Reality (AR) and Virtual Reality (VR)

AR and VR are poised to revolutionize how users engage with content, influencing future YouTube algorithms.

1: Enhanced User Experience

Immersive Content: Algorithms will prioritize immersive AR and VR content, providing users with highly engaging and interactive experiences.

Personalized AR/VR: Tailoring AR and VR experiences based on user preferences and past interactions.

2: New Content Formats

360-Degree Videos: Promoting and optimizing 360-degree video content to offer viewers a more comprehensive and interactive viewing experience.

Virtual Tours: Algorithms will highlight virtual tours and experiences, catering to users' growing interest in virtual travel and exploration.

9.2 User Privacy and Data Ethics

Evolving Standards for User Privacy and Data Protection

As concerns about privacy and data protection grow, YouTube must adapt its algorithms to comply with evolving standards.

1: Regulatory Compliance

GDPR and CCPA: Adhering to stringent data protection regulations like the General Data Protection Regulation (GDPR) and California Consumer Privacy Act (CCPA).

User Consent: Implementing clear and transparent consent mechanisms for data collection and usage.

2: Data Minimization

Limited Data Collection: Collecting only the data necessary to enhance user experience and improve content recommendations.

Anonymous Data Usage: Utilizing anonymized data to protect user identities while still leveraging insights for algorithm improvements.

Ethical Considerations in Algorithm Development

Ethical considerations are critical to ensuring that YouTube's algorithms operate fairly and responsibly.

1: Bias Mitigation

Fairness Audits: Regularly conducting fairness audits to identify and rectify any biases in algorithms.

Inclusive Training Data: Ensuring that training data is diverse and representative of all user demographics to prevent algorithmic bias.

2: Transparency and Accountability

Algorithmic Accountability: Establishing clear accountability for algorithmic decisions and their impacts on users.

Open Communication: Transparently communicating how algorithms work and the data they use to make decisions.

Balancing Personalization with User Consent

Personalization is key to user satisfaction, but it must be balanced with respect for user privacy and consent.

1: User Control

Preference Settings: Allowing users to control and customize their content recommendations and data usage preferences.

Opt-Out Options: Providing clear options for users to opt out of data collection and personalized recommendations.

2: Transparent Data Usage

Clear Explanations: Offering straightforward explanations of how user data is collected, used, and protected.

Feedback Mechanisms: Implementing feedback mechanisms for users to voice concerns and suggest improvements regarding data privacy and personalization.

9.3 Anticipating Future Trends

Predictions for Future Changes in Content Consumption

Understanding future trends in content consumption is vital for anticipating how YouTube algorithms will evolve.

1: Short-Form Content

Increased Popularity: The rise of short-form content, such as YouTube Shorts, will drive algorithmic adjustments to prioritize and promote these videos.

Micro-Engagement: Algorithms will focus on optimizing micro-engagement metrics, such as quick likes and shares, for short-form content.

2: Live Streaming

Real-Time Engagement: Algorithms will enhance real-time engagement features for live streams, promoting interactive content that fosters community building.

Event-Based Recommendations: Highlighting live events and streams based on user interests and real-time trends.

The Impact of Evolving User Behaviors on Algorithms

User behaviors are constantly changing, and algorithms must adapt to keep pace.

1: Content Binging

Series Optimization: Algorithms will increasingly recommend video series and playlists to cater to users' binge-watching habits.

Seamless Transitions: Enhancing user experience by providing seamless transitions between related videos and series.

2: Multi-Device Usage

Cross-Device Tracking: Algorithms will better track and integrate user interactions across multiple devices, ensuring consistent and personalized recommendations.

Adaptive Content Delivery: Optimizing content delivery based on the device being used, whether it's a smartphone, tablet, or smart TV.

Preparing for the Future as a Content Creator

Creators need to stay ahead of algorithmic trends to thrive on YouTube.

1: Staying Informed

Continuous Learning: Keeping up-to-date with YouTube's algorithm changes and best practices through resources like the Creator Academy and community forums.

Industry Insights: Following industry trends and adapting content strategies to align with emerging user preferences.

2: Innovative Content Strategies

Experimentation: Regularly experimenting with new content formats and styles to discover what resonates with audiences.

Audience Engagement: Fostering a strong connection with audiences through interactive features, personalized content, and responsive engagement.

3: Data-Driven Decisions

Analytics Tools: Utilizing YouTube Analytics and other tools to track performance, understand viewer behavior, and make informed decisions.

Feedback Integration: Actively seeking and integrating viewer feedback to improve content and align with audience expectations.

By leveraging emerging technologies, adhering to ethical standards, and anticipating future trends, YouTube's algorithms will continue to evolve, shaping the future of content creation and consumption on the platform.

Chapter 10
Practical Tips for Navigating YouTube Algorithms

10.1 Staying Updated with Algorithm Changes

Resources and Strategies for Keeping Up with Algorithm Updates

Staying informed about YouTube's algorithm changes is crucial for creators who want to maintain and grow their audience. Here are some effective ways to stay updated:

1: Official YouTube Channels and Blogs

YouTube Creator Blog: Regular updates and insights from YouTube about algorithm changes, new features, and best practices.

YouTube Creator Insider: A YouTube channel providing insider tips and explanations directly from the YouTube team.

2: Creator Academy

Courses and Tutorials: The YouTube Creator Academy offers free courses and tutorials on a wide range of topics, including how to optimize for the latest algorithm updates.

Webinars and Live Streams: Participating in live webinars and streams hosted by YouTube can provide direct access to the latest information and a chance to ask questions.

3: Industry News and Forums

Social Media Examiner: Websites like Social Media Examiner provide comprehensive articles on social media trends and algorithm updates.

Reddit and YouTube Community Forums: Engaging in discussions on Reddit's r/YouTube and other community forums can provide insights and tips from fellow creators.

The Importance of Continuous Learning and Adaptation

1: Adapting to Change

Flexible Strategies: Develop flexible content strategies that can be quickly adjusted in response to algorithm changes.

Experimentation: Regularly test new content formats, styles, and topics to see how they perform under the latest algorithm criteria.

2: Learning and Development

Skill Enhancement: Continuously improve your skills in video production, editing, and SEO to stay competitive.

Feedback Utilization: Use viewer feedback and analytics to identify areas for improvement and adapt your content accordingly.

Engaging with the YouTube Creator Community

1: Networking

Creator Meetups and Events: Attend YouTube-sponsored events and meetups to network with other creators and learn from their experiences.

Collaboration: Partner with other creators for collaborations that can help both parties learn and grow their audiences.

2: Online Communities

Facebook Groups and Discord Servers: Join groups and servers dedicated to YouTube creators for peer support and shared learning.

Mentorship Programs: Seek out mentorship opportunities from more experienced creators who can provide guidance and insights.

10.2 Practical Optimization Techniques

Actionable Tips for Optimizing Content Based on Current Algorithms

1: Keyword Research and Metadata

Effective Keywords: Use tools like Google Trends and YouTube's search suggest feature to identify popular keywords related to your content.

Optimized Metadata: Ensure that your video titles, descriptions, and tags are optimized with relevant keywords to improve search visibility.

2: Engagement Tactics

Compelling Thumbnails and Titles: Create eye-catching thumbnails and intriguing titles to increase click-through rates (CTR).

Call to Action (CTA): Include clear CTAs in your videos to encourage likes, comments, shares, and subscriptions.

3: Content Quality and Consistency

High Production Value: Invest in good equipment and editing software to enhance the production quality of your videos.

Regular Upload Schedule: Maintain a consistent upload schedule to keep your audience engaged and signal reliability to the algorithm.

Case Studies of Successful Optimization Strategies

1: MrBeast

Virality through Engagement: MrBeast's strategy includes high-stakes challenges and philanthropy, which generate massive engagement and virality.

Thumbnail and Title Optimization: Each video features compelling thumbnails and intriguing titles that draw viewers in.

2: Marques Brownlee (MKBHD)

Quality Content: Focus on high-quality, in-depth tech reviews that attract a dedicated audience.

Consistency: Regular uploads and a clear niche help maintain audience interest and algorithmic favor.

Tools and Analytics for Monitoring Performance

1: YouTube Analytics

Audience Insights: Use YouTube Analytics to understand viewer demographics, watch time, and engagement metrics.

Performance Tracking: Monitor how individual videos perform and identify trends in your content's success.

2: Third-Party Tools

TubeBuddy and VidIQ: Tools like TubeBuddy and VidIQ offer additional insights and optimization tips to enhance your content strategy.

Google Analytics: Integrate Google Analytics to get a broader view of your audience's behavior across different platforms.

10.3 Building a Resilient Content Strategy

Developing a Long-Term Content Strategy that Adapts to

Algorithm Changes

1: Content Diversification

Variety in Formats: Experiment with different content formats, such as tutorials, vlogs, live streams, and Shorts, to reach a wider audience.

Niche and Broad Topics: Balance niche-specific content with broader appeal topics to attract and retain diverse viewers.

2: Audience Engagement

Community Interaction: Actively engage with your audience through comments, community posts, and live streams to build a loyal community.

Feedback Incorporation: Use audience feedback to refine your content and ensure it meets their interests and expectations.

Diversifying Content and Revenue Streams

1: Multiple Platforms

Cross-Promotion: Promote your YouTube content on other social media platforms like Instagram, Twitter, and Facebook to reach a broader audience.

Alternative Channels: Consider creating multiple YouTube channels focused on different niches to diversify your content.

2: Monetization Strategies

Ad Revenue: Optimize your videos for ad placements to maximize revenue from YouTube's AdSense program.

Sponsorships and Brand Deals: Collaborate with brands for sponsored content and product placements.

Merchandise and Memberships: Launch merchandise lines and offer channel memberships to create additional revenue streams.

Building a Sustainable and Engaged Audience

1: Authenticity and Value

Authentic Content: Stay true to your voice and create content that genuinely resonates with your audience.

Value Proposition: Ensure your content provides value, whether through entertainment, education, or inspiration.

2: Consistency and Reliability

Regular Uploads: Stick to a consistent upload schedule to build trust and anticipation among your viewers.

Long-Term Vision: Develop a long-term vision for your channel, focusing on sustainable growth and audience loyalty.

By staying updated with algorithm changes, employing practical optimization techniques, and building a resilient content strategy, creators can successfully navigate YouTube's algorithms and achieve long-term success on the platform.

Closing Of the book

As we conclude **"How Algorithms Work on YouTube"**, we hope this journey has provided you with a deeper understanding of the complex and fascinating world of YouTube algorithms. By now, you should have a solid grasp of how these algorithms operate, from video discovery and recommendations to search ranking and engagement metrics.

Empowering Creators and Users

Whether you're a seasoned content creator or just starting out, knowledge is power. Understanding YouTube's algorithms equips you to create more engaging, discoverable content, and to build a loyal audience. For viewers, this insight offers a better understanding of how content is curated and presented, enhancing your overall YouTube experience.

The Dynamic Nature of Algorithms

One key takeaway from this book is the ever-evolving nature of algorithms. YouTube's algorithms are constantly updated to improve user experience, adapt to new trends, and incorporate advanced technologies. Staying informed about these changes is crucial for success on the platform. Regularly revisiting the principles and strategies outlined in this book will help you adapt and thrive in this dynamic environment.

A Future of Endless Possibilities

Looking ahead, the future of YouTube and its algorithms promises even more exciting developments. Emerging technologies such as AI, machine learning, AR, and VR will continue to shape the way content is created, shared, and consumed. By staying informed and adaptable, you can leverage these advancements to your advantage.

Your Role in the YouTube Ecosystem

As a creator, viewer, or marketer, you play an integral role in the YouTube ecosystem. Your engagement, feedback, and creativity drive the platform's evolution. Embrace the strategies and insights shared in this book to maximize your impact, contribute positively to the community, and achieve your goals on YouTube.

Final Thoughts

We hope this book has inspired you to take full advantage of the opportunities that YouTube offers. By mastering the art and science of algorithms, you can elevate your content, grow your audience, and make meaningful connections. Remember, the key to success lies in continuous learning, adaptation, and a genuine passion for your content and audience.

Thank you for embarking on this journey with us. We wish you the best of luck in your YouTube endeavors and look forward to seeing the incredible content you will create and share.

Sincerely,

FAISAL JAMIL

Description of the book

How Algorithms Work on YouTube: Understanding the Engine Behind the World's Largest Video Platform

YouTube, the world's largest video-sharing platform, operates on a complex system of algorithms that shape user experiences, influence content visibility, and drive engagement. "How Algorithms Work on YouTube" delves deep into these algorithms, providing a comprehensive guide for creators, marketers, and enthusiasts looking to understand and navigate this digital landscape.

Chapter 1: Introduction to YouTube Algorithms

The Evolution of YouTube Algorithms:

Trace the journey from basic popularity metrics to sophisticated machine learning models, highlighting key milestones and the role of user feedback.

Basic Concepts of Algorithms:

Understand the definition, types, and fundamental workings of algorithms, including how they process data and make decisions.

The Purpose of YouTube Algorithms:

Explore how YouTube algorithms enhance user experience, maximize engagement, and balance user satisfaction with business objectives.

Chapter 2: Video Discovery and Recommendations

How the Recommendation System Works:

Learn about the technology behind YouTube's recommendation engine, including factors influencing recommendations and the impact of user behavior.

Personalization and User Profiling:

Discover methods for creating user profiles and tailoring recommendations to individual preferences using demographic and geographic data.

Continuous Learning and Adaptation:

See how YouTube algorithms learn from new data and update recommendations in real-time to handle changing user behaviors and trends.

Chapter 3: Search Algorithms

Understanding YouTube Search:

Dive into the components of YouTube's search engine, including how search results are ranked and displayed.

Keyword Optimization and Metadata:

Master best practices for optimizing titles, descriptions, tags, and video transcripts to enhance searchability.

User Intent and Contextual Relevance:

Analyze how search algorithms interpret user intent and deliver relevant results, even for ambiguous queries.

Chapter 4: Engagement Metrics and Ranking

Key Engagement Metrics:

Define and explore the impact of views, likes, comments, and shares on video ranking.

Watch Time and Session Duration:

Understand the significance of watch time in algorithmic decisions and learn strategies to increase it.

User Interaction Signals:

Examine how likes, dislikes, comments, and click-through rates influence video rankings and algorithmic responses.

Chapter 5: Content Quality and Creator Reputation

Assessing Content Quality:

Discover criteria used by algorithms to evaluate content quality, balancing production value and viewer satisfaction.

Building Creator Reputation:

Learn how consistency, niche focus, and creator history impact algorithmic favorability.

Handling Content Violations and Demonetization:

Understand the consequences of content violations on ranking and monetization.

Chapter 6: Audience Development and Growth

Audience Retention Strategies:

Explore techniques for retaining viewers throughout videos and analyze retention graphs for insights.

Subscriber Growth and Engagement:

Discover factors influencing subscriber growth and strategies for engaging subscribers.

Community Building and Interaction:

Learn the importance of community engagement and best practices for fostering a loyal audience.

Chapter 7: Algorithmic Impact on Video Promotion

Trends and Virality:

Understand how algorithms detect and promote trending content and learn strategies for creating viral videos.

Cross-Promotions and Collaborations:

Explore the impact of cross-promotions and collaborations on algorithmic ranking.

Paid Promotions and Advertisements:

Gain insights into YouTube's ad algorithms and the role of paid promotions in organic ranking.

Chapter 8: Algorithm Transparency and Criticism

Transparency Efforts by YouTube:

Learn about YouTube's initiatives to increase algorithm transparency and its importance for trust and accountability.

Common Criticisms of YouTube Algorithms:

Explore issues related to bias, misinformation, and content diversity, with case studies of controversial algorithm decisions.

Balancing Algorithmic Decisions:

Understand the challenge of balancing diverse stakeholder interests and approaches to mitigate negative impacts.

Chapter 9: Future of YouTube Algorithms

Emerging Technologies in Algorithm Development:

Discover the role of AI, machine learning, predictive analytics, and AR/VR in future algorithm developments.

User Privacy and Data Ethics:

Explore evolving standards for user privacy, data protection, and ethical considerations in algorithm development.

Anticipating Future Trends:

Predict future changes in content consumption and prepare for evolving user behaviors as a content creator.

Chapter 10: Practical Tips for Navigating YouTube

Algorithms

Staying Updated with Algorithm Changes:

Find resources and strategies for keeping up with algorithm updates and continuous learning.

Practical Optimization Techniques:

Get actionable tips for optimizing content and tools for monitoring performance.

Building a Resilient Content Strategy:

Develop a long-term content strategy that adapts to algorithm changes, diversifies content, and builds a sustainable audience.

This book offers a blend of theoretical insights and practical strategies, equipping readers with the knowledge and tools needed to thrive on YouTube. Whether you are a seasoned creator or just starting, "How Algorithms Work on YouTube" will guide you through the intricacies of the platform's algorithms and help you achieve long-term success.